T0086942

Mary, Mother

Bob Chilcott

for SATB and piano or with organ and optional harp

vocal score

OXFORD
UNIVERSITY PRESS

OXFORD
UNIVERSITY PRESS

Great Clarendon Street, Oxford OX2 6DP,
United Kingdom

Oxford University Press is a department of the University of Oxford.
It furthers the University's objective of excellence in research, scholarship,
and education by publishing worldwide. Oxford is a registered trade mark of
Oxford University Press in the UK and in certain other countries

© Oxford University Press 2023

Bob Chilcott has asserted his right under the Copyright, Designs
and Patents Act, 1988, to be identified as the Composer of this Work

All rights reserved. No part of this publication may be reproduced,
stored in a retrieval system, or transmitted, in any form or by any means,
without the prior permission in writing of Oxford University Press

Permission to perform this work in public (except in the course of divine worship)
should normally be obtained from a local performing right licensing organization,
unless the owner or the occupier of the premises being used already holds
a licence from such an organization. Likewise, permission to make and
exploit a recording of these works should be obtained from a
local mechanical copyright licensing organization

Enquiries concerning reproduction outside the scope of the above
should be directed to the Music Rights Department, Oxford University Press,
at music.permissions.uk@oup.com or at the address above

ISBN 978-0-19-356427-5

Music and text origination by Katie Johnston
Printed in Great Britain on acid-free paper by
Halstan & Co. Ltd, Amersham, Bucks.

Contents

1. A Child in Galilee 5
2. Carpentry Carol 13
3. After the angel 21
4. Walking Carol 26
5. Dear heart 30
6. Hymn 36

Authors' note

Mary, Mother is a sequence of six carols that articulates the role of Mary in the Christmas story, very much from the human perspective. The author, Georgia Way, has written new, warm, and thoughtful texts that she introduces here:

These six carol texts came into being on the premise that Mary might be one of the best-known figures in the Christian world, but she might also be one of the least understood. Could the serene image of the Mother of God have become distant to us through her familiarity?

The challenge, then, was to find a way to make Mary's experiences, as a human woman, emotionally relevant to audiences today. This is perhaps why the sycamore tree became a central image. In the Bible, *Ficus sycomorus* is a way to see further, a way to see Jesus as he approaches. For me, this reflects one of the roles that music plays in our lives: a way to see further into emotional and spiritual truth.

If the sycamore casts a note of doubt, of instability, into Mary's emerging adulthood in the first of these six carols, then the remaining five work to resolve that instability. It is fitting to me that the sycamore should return in the final carol, a hymn to the regenerative power of the human spirit.

The carols that make up *Mary, Mother* can be performed individually or as a set. The accompaniment in this vocal score is designed to be played on the piano. The work was conceived with organ and harp accompaniment, and a full score and parts for this version are available for digital download.

Mary, Mother was written for St Martin's Voices and their Director, Andrew Earis, who gave the first performance at St Martin-in-the-Fields, London, on 18 December 2022.

Bob Chilcott and Georgia Way, June 2023

Duration: *c.*17 mins

For Andrew Earis and St Martin's Voices, St Martin-in-the Fields, London;
commissioned with the generous support of an anonymous donor

Mary, Mother

1. A Child in Galilee

Georgia Way (b. 1992) **BOB CHILCOTT**

Music © Oxford University Press 2023. Text © Georgia Way. Reproduced by kind permission.

Printed in Great Britain

OXFORD UNIVERSITY PRESS, MUSIC DEPARTMENT, GREAT CLARENDON STREET, OXFORD OX2 6DP
The Moral Rights of the Composer have been asserted. Photocopying this copyright material is ILLEGAL.

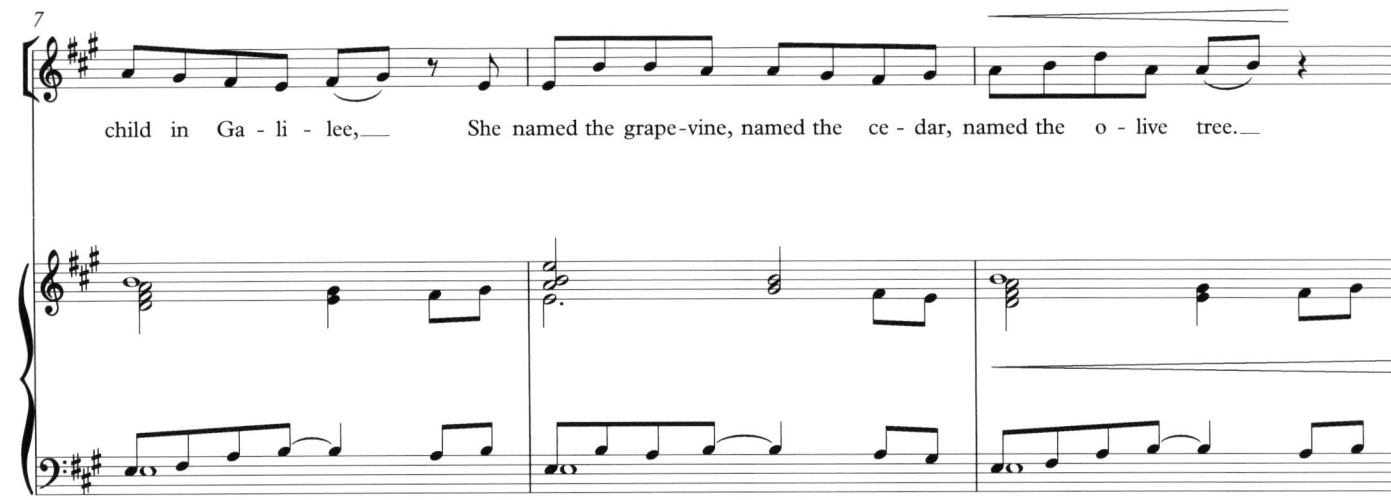
7
child in Ga - li - lee,
She named the grape-vine, named the ce - dar, named the o - live tree.

'Raise your voice, young Ma - ry,' called out the o - live tree,
'For
10
mp
mf
S.
A.
'Raise your voice,' called out the o - live tree,
'One
T.
B.
mp
mf
'Raise your voice,' called out the o - live tree,
mp
mf

one day I will crown you as Queen of Ga - li -
12
mp
day I will crown you.'
mp
- lee.'
14
p
p
mp
17
mp
A young girl, a girl in
T. & B. unis.
mp
When Ma - ry was a young girl, a girl in Ga - li - lee, She

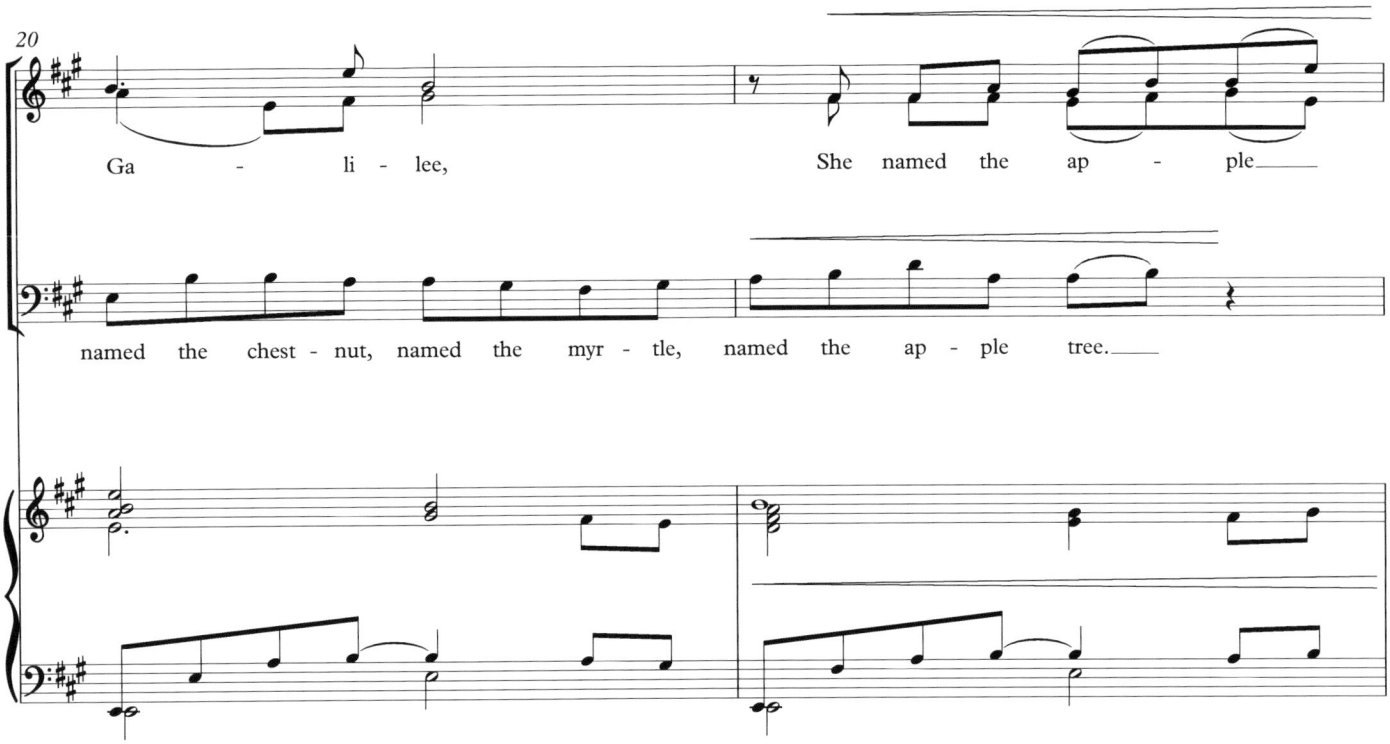
20
Ga - li - lee,
She named the ap - ple
named the chest - nut, named the myr - tle, named the ap - ple tree.

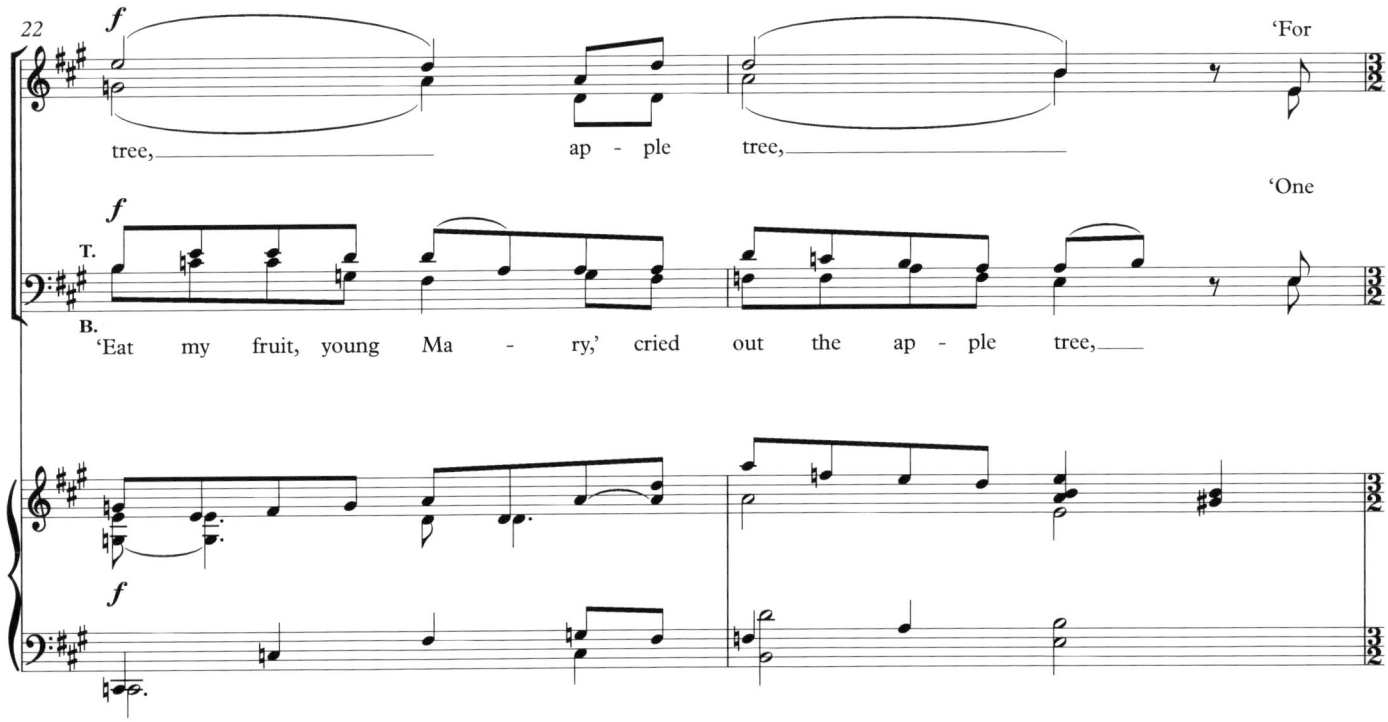
22
f
tree,
ap - ple tree,
'For
f
T.
B.
'Eat my fruit, young Ma - ry,' cried out the ap - ple tree,
'One
f

24
one day I will kneel to you as
day I will kneel to you as Queen of Ga - li - lee.'
27
mf
grown in Ga - li - lee,
When Ma - ry was a wo - man, all grown in Ga - li -
mf
mf

30
She sought the shade of a sy - ca - more, a sigh - ing, sigh - ing
-lee, She sought the shade of a sigh - - ing
sigh - - ing,

33
sy - ca - more tree. 'If you name me, if you
mp
sy - ca - more tree. 'If you name me, if you
mf
tree. 'Ma - ry, if you name me, if you
mf
mp
sigh - - ing tree. 'If you name me,
mp

tie your - self to me, You'll ne - ver name the Tree of Life, as
35
mf
tie your-self to me, You'll
ne - ver name the Tree of Life, as
tie your - self to me, You'll
mf
mf
tie your - self to me, You'll ne - ver name the Tree of Life, as

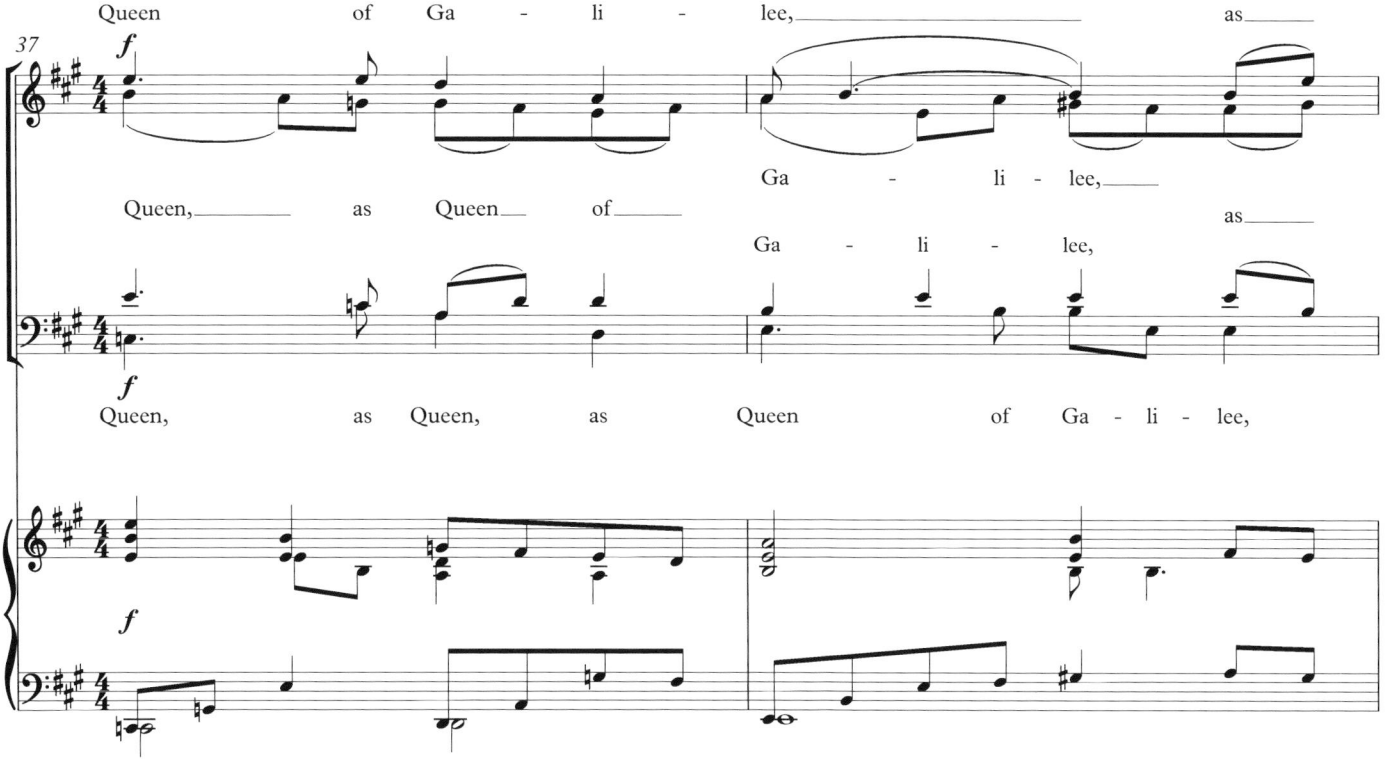
Queen of Ga - li - lee, as
37
f
Ga - li - lee,
Queen, as Queen of
as
Ga - li - lee,
f
Queen, as Queen, as Queen of Ga - li - lee,
f

39
Queen, as Queen of Ga - li - lee,
Queen, as Queen of Ga - li - lee, as Queen of
Queen, as Queen, as Queen of Ga - li - lee,
42
mp
rit.
Ga - li - lee,
mp
rit.
mp
slower
46
p
as Queen of Ga - li - lee.
p
slower
p

2. Carpentry Carol

13
sing, sy - ca - more, sing! Sing, sy - ca - more, sing!
f
Build - ing a crib for the fu - ture king.
mf
17
Build - ing a crib for the fu - ture king.
mf
mf
21
T.
B.
mf
She fell for his hands as gnarled as old roots, his

25
mind as young as green tim - ber.
All the while he
29
S.
A.
he hummed to the tune:
O sing, sy - ca - more, sing!
T.
B.
hummed to the tune:
f
33
Me - lo - dies carved for the heav'n - ly
Sing, sy - ca - more, sing!
Me - lo - dies carved for the heav'n - ly

37
king.
41
mf dolce espress.
Fall - ing in love, fall - ing in
mf dolce espress.
Fall - ing in love is ham - mer and saw,
mf dolce espress.
45
love, feel - ing safe,
chi - sel and knife, feel - ing safe, safe,

49
f
feel - ing safe in a house on fire,
f
f
and want - ing more.
53
mp
cresc.
and want - ing, want - ing more. O
mp
cresc.
57
sing, sy - ca - more, sing! Sing, sy - ca - more, sing!
mp cresc.

Na - za - reth waits
61
f
Na - za - reth waits for the song, the song of the
f
f
65
king.
mf
69
S.
A.
mf
Ma - ry gave her pro - mise that day to the

73
S.
A.
man with the ten - der heart and hands,
carv - ing joy with a
T.
B.
mf
77
f
plane and a lathe.
O sing, sy - ca - more, sing!
f
f
81
Craft - ing the world for our heav'n - ly,
Sing, sy - ca - more, sing!
Craft - ing the world for our heav'n - ly,

85
heav'n - ly king. O sing, sy - ca - more, sing!
f
89
Craft - ing the world for our heav'n - ly
Sing, sy - ca - more, sing! Craft - ing the world for our heav'n - ly
93
mf
rit.
king.
mf
rit.
mf
mp
RH

3. *After the angel*

9
mp
you have ta - ken a - way the key, ta - ken the key to my
mp
mp
12
and the door o - ver - sha - dows my
poco espress.
poco rit.
hus - band's house and the door o - ver - sha - dows my
poco espress.
poco rit.
poco rit.
a tempo
15
p dolce
heart. And the Lord ap - peared, and
p dolce
a tempo
p dolce

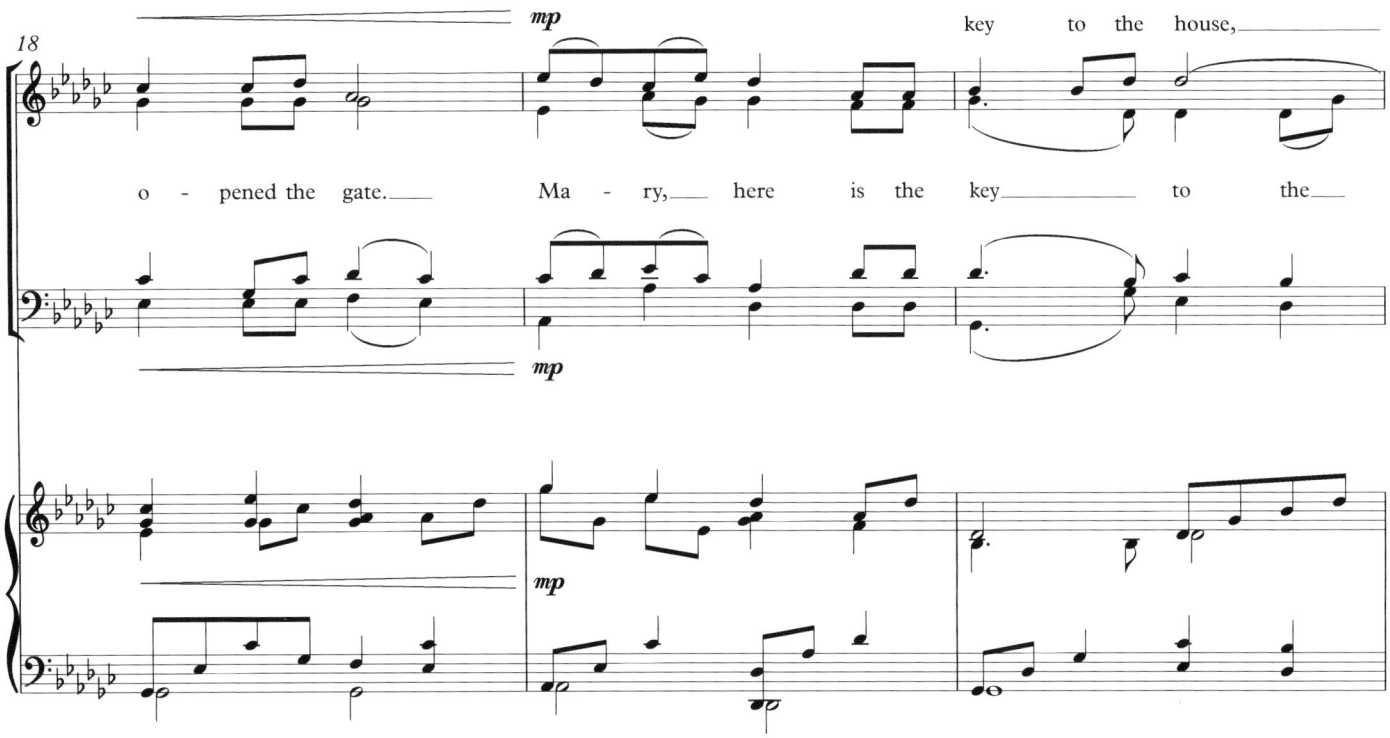
18
mp
key to the house,
o - pened the gate.
Ma - ry,
here is the key
to the
mp
mp

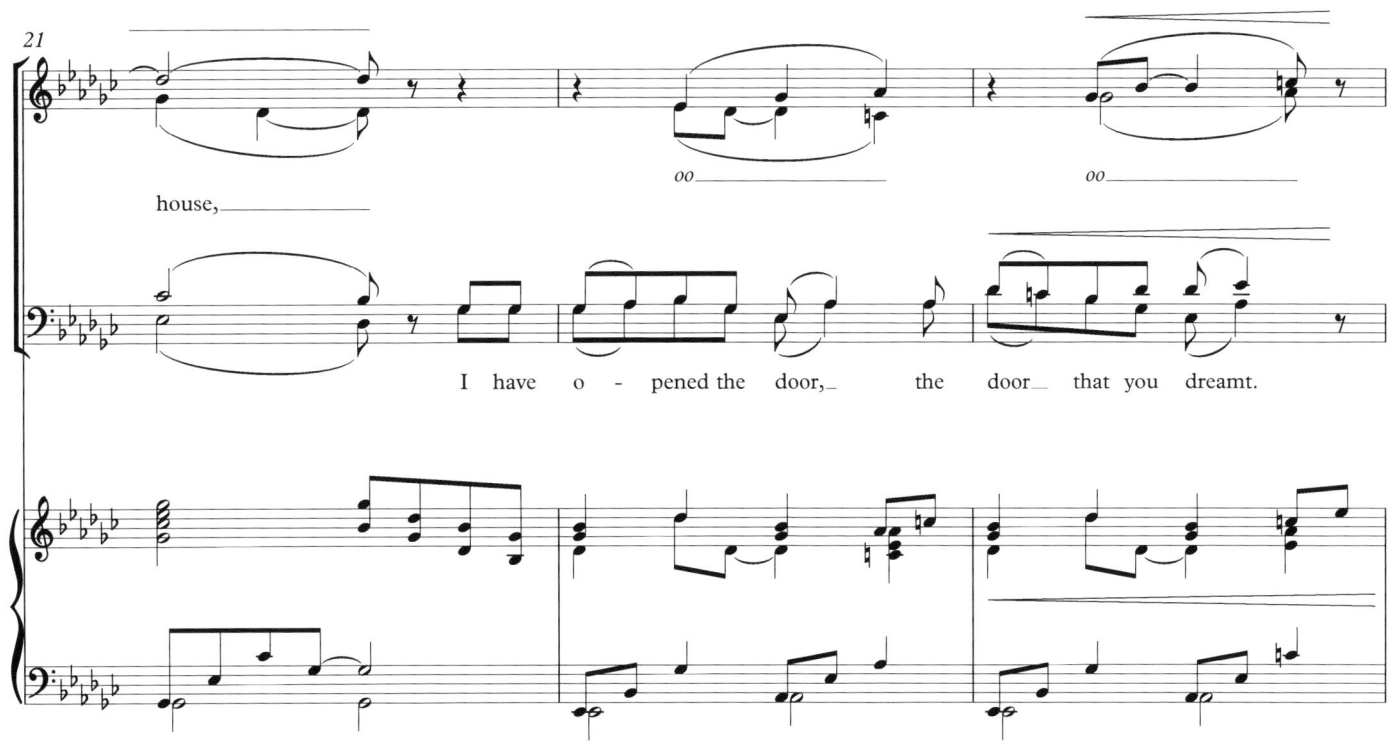
21
house,
oo
oo
I have o - pened the door,
the door
that you dreamt.

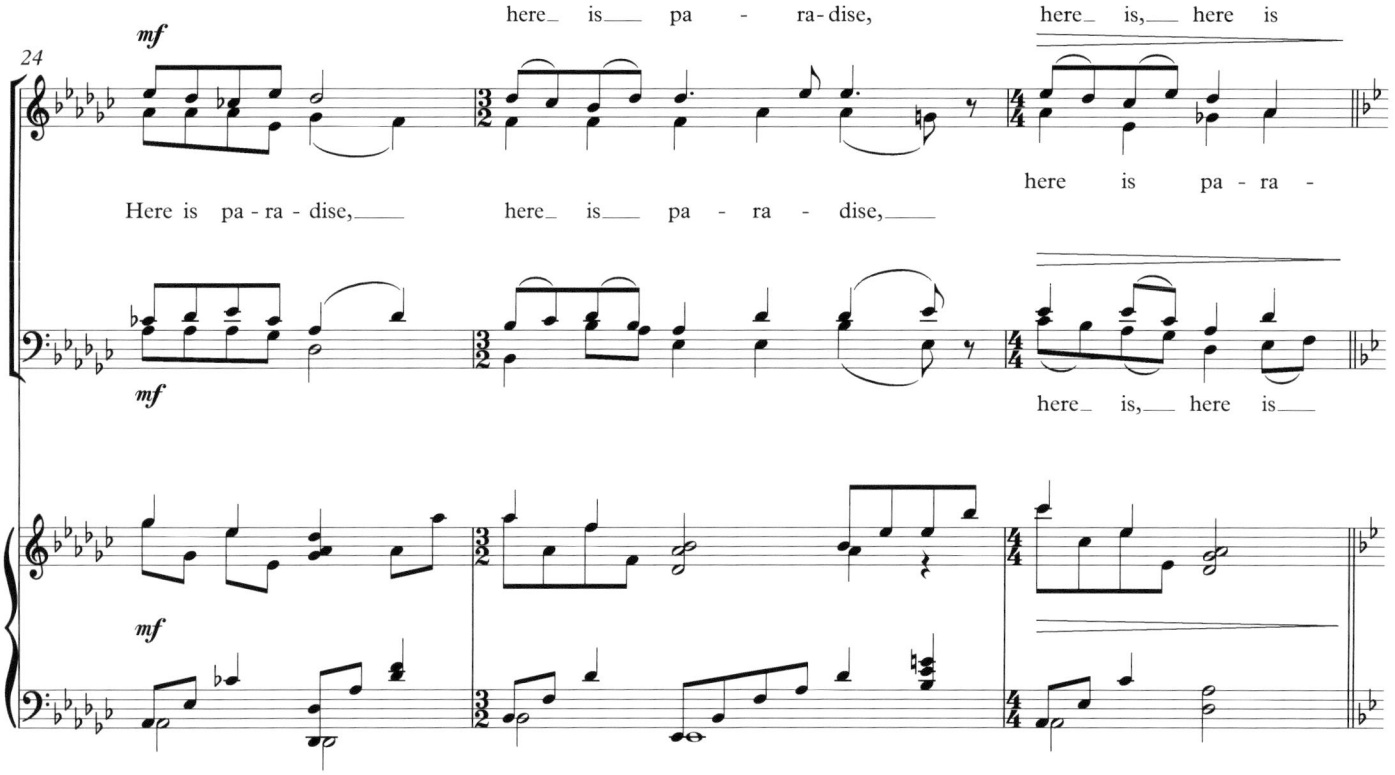
24
mf
here is pa - ra-dise, here is, here is
here is pa - ra -
Here is pa - ra - dise, here is pa - ra - dise,
here is, here is
mf
mf

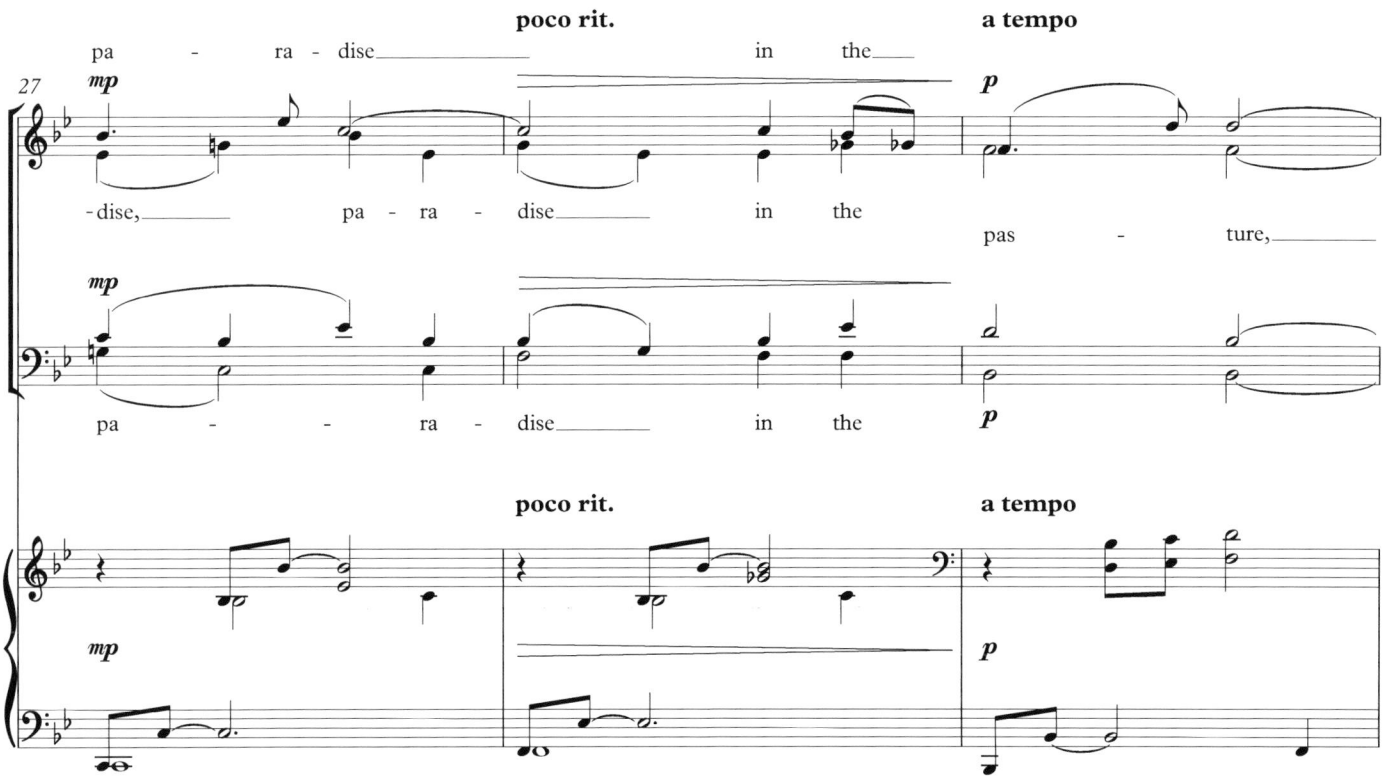
27
mp
pa - ra - dise in the
poco rit.
a tempo
p
-dise, pa - ra - dise in the
pas - ture,
mp
pa - - ra - dise in the
p
poco rit.
a tempo
mp
p

30
the key to hea - ven,
and to - day I give you the key, the key, the key to
34
to hea - ven
poco rit.
a little slower
heav'n, to hea - ven in the hu - man heart, the key to hea - ven
poco rit.
a little slower
38
rit.
in the hu - man heart.
rit.
p
pp

4. Walking Carol

13
poco cresc.
mf
road, end-less, end - less, end - less road.
poco cresc.
mf
Two for bread to eat as we go, Three for the times we've lost our way, Four, cold and hun-gry all
poco cresc.
mf
16
mf
Five for the rain that trou-bles our eyes,
mp
day.
mf
End - less
mp
mf
19
Six for Ma - ry, fright-ened and shy, Se - ven for Cae - sar in far - off Rome,
end - less road, end - less
road, end - less, end - - - less

21
Eight for wish - ing we could all go home.
road, end - less road.
25
f
Nine for the months of growth and pain, Ten for the cen-sus and tax - es to pay, E -
f
f
27
ff
- le - ven for Jo - seph, wor-ried and tired, And twelve for the joy of the un - born child,
ff
ff

29
f
un - born child.
f
f
mp
33
poco rit.
a tempo
S. & A unis. p
Lord, the road to hap - pi - ness is long as win - ter's night.
T. & B. unis.
p
poco rit.
a tempo
p
37
poco rit.
a little slower
Send a star to bright - en us.
poco rit.
a little slower
pp

5. Dear heart

Lullaby ♩ = c.60
SOPRANO SOLO
SOPRANO ALTO
p dolce
Dear heart, dear heart.
TENOR BASS
p dolce
Dear heart, dear heart.
Lullaby ♩ = c.60
PIANO
p dolce
con Ped.
4
p dolce espress.
S. SOLO
Do you re-mem-ber be-fore you were here? The house and the sta-ble, the
7
turn of the year? Last night I lost my heart to a star.

10
S. SOLO
Lul - ly, lul - ly, lul - la.
Now,
S. A.
pp
Dear heart, dear
T. B.
pp
Dear heart,
pp
13
heart, you are sleep - ing and hard - ly stir.
Qui - et - ened by frank - in -
heart,
dear heart, dear heart, dear,

16
mp
-cense and myrrh.
Lul - ly, lul - la, lul - ly,
mp
dear heart. Last night I lost my heart to a star.
mp
mp
19
mf ma dolce
lul - ly, lul - ly, lul - la.
Lul - ly, lul - ly, lul - la.
mf ma dolce
Lul - ly, lul - ly, lul - la.
mf ma dolce
mf ma dolce

22
S.
A.
Sheep and shep - herds, ox - en and kings: Mor - tal the gifts that
T.
B.
25
Beth - le - hem brings. Your star - light has car - ried my
27
mp
heart a - way. O love - ly child,
mp
mp
poco rit.
lul - ly, lul -
p
lul - ly, lul -
p
poco rit.
p

30
a tempo
p
S. SOLO
E - ven while sleep - ing, e - ven so new,
- lay.
S. A.
- lay.
T. B.
a tempo
34
mp
Now and for - ev - er my heart is you. Last night I lost my
mp
Last night I lost my
mp
mp

poco rit.
37
heart to a star. Lul - ly, lul - ly, lul - la,
Lul - ly, lul - ly, lul - la.
heart to a star. Lul - ly, lul - ly, lul - ly, lul -
poco rit.
a little slower
40
p
rit.
lul - ly, lul - ly, lul - la.
pp
Dear heart, dear heart.
- la.
Dear heart, dear heart.
a little slower
rit.

6. Hymn

Warmly ♩ = c.80
SOPRANO
ALTO
S. & A. unis.
mp
In my heart is a sy - ca - more tree,
TENOR
BASS
Warmly ♩ = c.80
PIANO
mp
con Ped.
5
S.
A.
Tend it, La - dy, Heav'n - ly Queen. Sow the seed of love to - day,
9
S.
A.
Nur - ture ev - 'ry soul, I pray.
mf
O sing al - le - lu - ia! In ex -
T. & B. unis.
T.
B.
mf
mf

13
-cel - sis glo - ri - a!
Queen of hea - ven,
17
S.
A.
Pray for me,
for ev-'ry sy-ca-more tree,
pray for me,
Pray for ev - 'ry
sy-ca-more tree,
Pray for ev - 'ry
21
ev-'ry flow'r-ing bud,
Ev-'ry mo - ther,
ev - 'ry child.
f
O sing al - le -
T.
B.
flow'r-ing bud,
Ev - 'ry mo - ther,
ev - 'ry child.
f
f

25
-lu - ia! In ex - cel - sis glo - ri - a!

SOPRANO DESCANT
29
f
Hear the an - gels sing on high, 'Christ the Lord is born this
ALL OTHER VOICES
f
Hear the an - gels sing on high, 'Christ the Lord is born this night!'

33
night!' Born to save the world from sin, Ev - 'ry heart shall
Born to save the world from sin, Ev - 'ry heart shall
poco rit.
a little slower
36
ff
let him in. King of Kings, al - le - lu - ia! In ex -
ff
let him in. King of Kings, al - le - lu - ia! In ex -
poco rit.
a little slower
ff
39
rit.
- cel - sis glo - ri - a!
- cel - sis glo - ri - a!
rit.